The Ultimate Self-Directed IRA

Using Self-Directed IRAs & Solo 401ks To Invest
In Real Estate, Bitcoin, Ethereum,
Cryptocurrencies, Gold, Private Businesses,
Startups, Exotics & Much More

…In Plain English:

Quick No-Nonsense Guide

Jeff Astor

Contents

Chapter 1

Your Author: A Man in the Trenches

My name is Jeff Astor. For five years now, I've been speaking daily to people from all walks of life and in all 50 states about the basics, as well as the intricacies, of Self-Directed IRAs (SD IRAs). My job has been to answer all their questions about these powerful retirement vehicles – and to do so in the clearest, shortest possible way. That's not to say I don't give everyone all the time they need to achieve clarity. But I've done this so often for so long, for thousands of people, that I know how to cut to the chase and explain things in plain English.

That's why I can describe this book as a "Quick, No-Nonsense Guide" to SD IRAs. At the end, you won't know everything, of course, but you'll know enough to know what you don't know, and where to find it. You'll know who to ask to get any particulars of your situation clarified.

Having said that, for the sake of full disclosure, I've been able to communicate daily with thousands of people (more than 10,000) because I work for one of the leading firms in the self-directed field, Broad Financial. Nevertheless, I will try to be as objective and generic as possible. I always tell people that they should do their own research; they shouldn't take my word for it or rely exclusively on what they read on the internet or in a book. "Do your homework," I always say.

What I can provide you with is a perspective from a man in the trenches. Every day, people from all over the US – young and not-quite-young; east coast, west coast and Midwest – contact Broad Financial. Some of them have done their research and have only a few pointed questions of an advanced nature. Some are rank beginners. Some are financial planners, accountants and attorneys. Some are everyday Americans – men, women, mothers, fathers, grandfathers and grandmothers. Some are sophisticated metropolitans. Some are intelligent, down-to-earth retirees who have definite ideas but want straight answers. Some know exactly what they want to invest in. Some have no idea.

Whoever they are, I've fielded their questions. And whoever you are, I've put together this no-nonsense guide to get you up to speed quickly about one of the most powerful retirement vehicles on the planet. A vehicle that remains one of America's best-kept secrets.

Which leads me to the next chapter...

Chapter 2

The Big Secret: The Self-Directing Revolution

One of the most common questions I get is: If this is such a powerful retirement vehicle, how come I've never heard of it until recently? And why don't more people know about it?

The answer is straight-forward: The brokerages and investment houses that hold your retirement money are not happy at the prospect of you moving your money out of their hands and into your own control. They lose commissions. They lose income.

That's not to say that they're dishonest, scheming liars. No. It's just not in their purview to learn about these plans and recommend them to their clients. One can assume that most of the employees who man these firms are as unaware about the existence of SD IRAs as the rest of the population.

Another reason that self-directed plans are not so well-known is that it took a 1986 lawsuit that wasn't adjudicated until 1996 (and issued in 2000 to the IRS field agents) before the IRS acknowledged that individuals have the right to self-direct with checkbook control. That means that for 22 years (since 1974 when the concept of IRAs was first created), people thought they were forced to keep their money at brokerage and investment houses. SD IRAs came late to the retirement party. That's why most people don't know of them, and those who do, ask why they never heard about them beforehand.

The veil of ignorance is so pervasive that even many otherwise experienced accountants and financial people don't know about them. They went to school and built up their careers before the landmark court decision. That has led to the irony that older more-established people in the finance world tend to know less about SD IRAs than younger financial advisors.

Either way, SD IRAs are here. And they've been so for a while.

They received an upsurge in interest after the crash-recession-depression (whatever you want to call it) of 2008 and 2009. People got killed on Wall Street. That led many to seek other ways to invest. In fact, that's how Broad Financial came about. Its owners lost about 40% of the value of their retirement portfolios. They asked themselves why they were so invested in Wall Street. They knew real estate. Was there a way to use their retirement money in real estate? That's when they discovered SD IRAs for themselves. Then they told family and friends about them. Then strangers. Before they knew it, they had a new business.

How many Americans self-direct? Some estimate that Americans have between $16 trillion to well over $20 trillion in retirement plans! Yes, trillion. Of that, estimates are that maybe only 1% to 2% self-direct.

Is an SD IRA for everyone? No. Nevertheless, some suggest that at least 10% of Americans can benefit from self-directing. The bottom line is that there are a lot of people that still don't know about SD IRAs – people who can benefit from them in ways they never realized possible.

If self-directing your retirement is a revolution, then we are only at the beginning.

Note: "Self-directed" is sometimes used by brokerages and Wall Street firms to refer to their clients' ability to invest in any type of stocks and mutual funds on their own. That's not true self-

direction. In the truest sense, it means the ability to go beyond Wall Street and into what is commonly called "alternative investments," which includes but is not limited to real estate (not a real estate stock like a REIT, but actual property).

Chapter 3

Why Are People Self-Directing? What's the Advantage?

There are many, but let me break it down into three large categories: Diversification, Balance and Opportunity.

Diversification

No one knows when the next recession will hit. I have a friend who is an economist. He works for a major international bank with other major-league economists. He told me that the economists have a joke among themselves: "They predicted nine of the last three recessions…"

We all know some type of recession, correction (whatever you want to call it) is coming. The market never proceeds in a straight line. We don't know when it will happen, but it's not just scare-mongering to say it will happen.

And we don't know how big it will be. Will it be a little cough? A tremor? An earthquake? Or what Californian's call the "Big One"? No one knows. But saying it can never happen or will never happen is naïve.

Is there a hedge against such an event? In many cases, yes: self-direction. In this sense, a self-directed retirement plan is another word for diversification.

And not diversification in the way Wall Street means it. Yes, there's value to having a diverse selection of stocks, bonds and mutual funds. But, as the saying goes: When the tide rises, all the boats rise; when it lowers, all the boats sink.

True diversification would include, for instance, actual real estate. Yes, real estate can lose value. It's prone to the ebb and flow of the economy like everything else. But it's "real" estate. It's not a piece of paper indicating value.

Years ago, my wife received an inheritance from a relative in the form of shares in a major Canadian utility company. When she received it, we thought about selling the shares and using the cash for a different investment. We didn't. Within a few months, this "rock-solid" Canadian company went belly up. We were left with literally nothing but the paper telling us how many shares worth zero we had.

If we had plunked that cash into a piece of real estate, it too could have lost all its value. But with real estate, chances are that sooner or later it will come back. And when it does you won't be holding a worthless piece of paper, but "real" estate.

Again, nothing is guaranteed, but that's the idea of diversifying. True diversification means going beyond Wall Street and its rising and descending tides. By all means, keep some of your funds in the market, if you want. However, if you want to truly diversify your IRA, you need to think about having some alternative assets (real estate is only one such type) in your portfolio. You can only do that with a self-directed retirement plan.

Balance

The second major reason that people consider SD IRAs is balance. They just made nice money in the market. They have extra cash. Now they want to rebalance their portfolios. It's the wise thing to do. All financial advisors advocate it.

Then they recall that they once heard about something called a Self-Directed IRA, which gives them the ability to invest in tangible assets, not just paper. Now that would really be a way to balance their portfolios.

"Rebalancers" are not so concerned about a recession. They're protected (or at least they think they are). They look to alternative assets as a means of wealth creation and expansion. They want to rebalance.

Opportunity

The third major type of person interested in Self-Directed IRA is one who has watched their 401k stay the same (or whittle away) over the years. The only one getting rich off it is their broker or brokerage. They heard that they can make money in alternative investments. That's when they started their research into SD IRAs.

Those are only three of the reasons. There are others. For example: They received an inherited IRA. Or a friend has a great opportunity in real estate or a startup company. They think it's cool.

Whatever the reason, they realize there is a revolution going on and they want to join it in their own way and on their own terms.

Chapter 4

What Can I Invest In?

Okay, I've mentioned "alternative investments." What are examples of alternative investments? What does an SD IRA allow me to invest in?

There are three basic categories: Real estate, almost everything else and "exotics."

Real Estate

Real estate is the most common asset people with SD IRAs invest in. There's an ancient adage that advises people to have at least one-third of their assets in real estate. It's still true today.

As noted above, real estate is "real." It's not paper. Even if everything else crashes, you have something tangible that, chances are, sooner or later will regain its value – and then some.

Also, people who know how to make money in real estate typically make much better returns than the average investor can achieve on Wall Street. Some of my clients have told me that, without trying, they make an 8% to 10% return in real estate. Others have said that they can regularly make 20%. A few others have told me more – even a lot more. Whatever it is, they are better at real estate than Wall Street.

Cryptocurrencies

When I originally published this book in early 2017, using an IRA to purchase bitcoin and other cryptocurrencies was rare. It was barely a blip on the radar. I only mentioned it in passing, including it in the "Exotics" section below.

That all changed by the second quarter of 2017. Cryptocurrencies are now the second-most common alternative asset and rising in popularity every day, even threatening to dethrone real estate as number one! It's been an incredible run, and it only seems to be gaining momentum. Read ahead, Chapter 6, for real stories of real people I've helped set up plans who have made incredible gains inside their SD IRAs (and Solo 401ks) with bitcoin and other cryptos.

Tier-Twos

The second most common category of alternative investments includes investing in assets such as precious metals (e.g. actual gold, silver), tax liens, shares in private companies, startups and businesses. It also includes people earning tax-sheltered (or tax-free) interest from hard money loans. I remember one fellow who told me that he made bridge loans of about $500,000 with something like 10% interest. Some of these loans were for six months or less. He was now interested in doing that with his retirement money. Whereas before he would have to give some of his capital gains to Uncle Sam, with an SD IRA he could keep it and reinvest it.

That, by the way, is one of the advantages of investing with an SD IRA. In the above example, this fellow turned $500,000 into $550,000 in a few months. But he had to pay 40% on his gains, reducing his $50,000 profit to $30,000. For the next deal he had $530,000 to lend. If he did it with his IRA, he would have all $550,000 for the next time. Over time, after completing more deals, he will have a lot more capital to make money with. Yes, he will have to pay taxes when he retires, but the average retiree will be in a lower tax bracket and be taking out only a portion of his IRA.

Another type of "tier-two" alternative investment I learned from my clients is the emerging field of crowdfunding or peer-to-peer platforms. I remember a client who told me how happy he was with his investments at a peer-to-peer lending website. The site attracts borrowers and lenders. The potential borrowers are vetted and, if approved, they are given a risk-rating and uploaded to the website. That allows private individuals to become lenders to these people. My client would make thousands of loans in small amounts (e.g. $50–100) to spread out his risk. The bottom line is that a self-directed IRA would allow him to invest in this peer-to-peer website.

There are also peer-to-peer real estate and other investment websites that work similarly.

Let me be clear that I'm not endorsing any of them, but merely letting you know what some of my clients have invested their SD IRAs into.

Another tier-two investment is "private placements." These include hedge funds, private equity, startups and private companies. As we'll see ahead, these are probably more ideal for a custodial SD IRA than a checkbook IRA (see Chapter 7), but they can be very powerful.

I remember speaking to a doctor who had $125,000 and wanted to use it to get in on the ground floor at a pharmaceutical company that was researching a new drug. He was hoping to make millions off it. That's a private placement.

Many people call up saying that they know a friend who has been making a killing in real estate. They want to invest their IRA with him. Can they do it with an SD IRA? The answer is, of course, yes.

One of the most popular investments is precious metals. We're not talking about an ETF or stock that represents gold, silver or the like. We're talking about actual metals – bars, coins, etc. These are especially popular when people are nervous about the economy. In most cases, the precious metals are held at an approved depository through an IRA custodian, such as Brinks or the Delaware Depository. In some cases, you can take actual physical possession of them. (See Chapter 15, "Rapid-Fire Q & A" for more.)

Exotics

This brings me to the last category (in some ways my favorite), which I call "exotic" investments.

One of my more interesting calls was from a man who wanted to know if he could set up an SD IRA to invest in Arabian racehorses. Full disclosure: I know nothing about Arabian racehorses. I still don't, but he gave me a basic education: You look for a foal from good stock. You might spend a couple of years paying for its food, lodging, grooming, etc. Chances are your investment will not pan out. But if it does – if you get a real stud horse – you're off to the races…

That's one of the nice things about my job. I get to learn what others are thinking about making money in.

Other "exotics" I've encountered include a young Hollywood film producer who had people interested in using their IRA money to invest in her film. The answer, of course, is they could.

Another caller wanted to know if they could invest in a treasure park, which is a place where families come to look for buried treasure. The answer: Yes.

One of my colleagues had someone who came on board to use his IRA to invest in a zoo. Yes, a zoo.

Another quasi-exotic is foreign currency. When I first began, numerous people were calling to see if they could invest in Iraqi dinars. Yes, they could, I told them. Of course, that was before the rise of ISIS. Since then, we haven't had many inquiries about investing in Iraqi dinars.

Again, for all things, do your research. Don't jump into the alternative investment wagon just because it's "alternative." But if it makes sense for you, the SD IRA is the way to go.

Chapter 5

What Can't I Invest In?

This will be a short chapter. There are only two assets you can't use an IRA to invest in: collectibles and life insurance [IRC Section 408(a)(3)].

Collectibles are assets such as antiques, artwork, rugs, gems, stamps, alcoholic beverages and coins (numismatics). It is prohibited to use your IRA to invest in collectibles. If you do, the amount invested is considered distributed in the year invested and you may have to pay a 10% additional tax on early distributions.

Sometimes the definition of collectible is unclear. One fellow told me that he bought old cars, fixed them up and resold them. He asked me if he could buy a 1967 Mustang with his IRA. I said, I didn't know about cars, but if the value was based on its "collectability," then it would probably be a no-go. He argued with me. I reiterated that I didn't know cars like he did, but the litmus test was if people were buying them for their antique value or not. I then advised him, as I do in all such gray areas, to consult with an ERISA attorney. (ERISA attorneys specialize in retirement law; more on that below.)

I had a similar conversation with a person who had more than $1 million worth of baseball cards. I said it seemed to me that they were collectibles. Why else would you pay more for a Mickey Mantle card in mint condition? In the end, I advised him to speak to an ERISA attorney.

Prohibited Transactions

Collectibles and life insurance are the two types of assets you can't use your IRA to invest in. However, all assets are off limits if you invest in a way the IRS considers self-dealing; in a way that's not an "arm's length transaction." The common term is "prohibited transactions."

For instance, you can't use your IRA to invest in a property you already own. Similarly, even if you never owned a property, you can't buy it with your IRA and then make personal use of it.

Once, a guy on the east coast called me up with a great opportunity to use his IRA to purchase a ski lodge in Colorado. It would be a money-maker for him. But he wanted to use it to ski there. I told him that's prohibited. But, he said, it would only be one weekend per month. No go, I told him. Even one night would be in violation.

Similarly, people call up saying they want to buy a rental, but sleep in it one night every now and then. Also, a no-go.

Disqualified Persons

Another classification of "thou shalt nots" in SD IRAs is what is commonly called "disqualified persons." These are people you can't interact with even if all the other factors are okay; even if, for example, it's a new property that you have no intention of making personal benefit of. If it's with one of the people the IRS considers disqualified you can't use your IRA for it.

Many people call me and say that they're aware the rules of disqualified persons forbid them from doing business with relatives. I tell them that's not strictly correct. Some relatives you can have dealings with. The IRS limited the definition of disqualified persons to *lineal* ancestors and descendants. So, for instance, you can't buy property from (or sell to) your spouse, parents or grandparents. You can't make deals with your children and grandchildren. But brothers and sisters are okay; so are aunts and uncles, nieces and nephews, cousins, etc. Yes, you can use your IRA to buy your brother's house. Not disqualified.

Other examples of disqualified persons include: The fiduciary of the Self-Directed IRA and anyone else that provides services to the account/plan (e.g. accountant, financial advisor).

Another important point to know about is that it is prohibited to have dealings with any entity (e.g. corporation, partnership, LLC, etc.) that is owned 50% or more by disqualified persons. For instance, if you and a partner own an LLC equally, 50%–50%, that LLC is off limits to your IRA. That's also true if you and your spouse, or you and a child or you and several children combined, own 50% or more. That LLC is off limits to your IRA. However, if you or any combination of disqualified persons own less than 50%, then it is possible to make an investment into the LLC. (In such cases, it's always good to speak to a self-directed specialist.)

The rules governing prohibited transactions are not overly complicated. The basics are easy enough to understand. Just make sure that, if you're ever unsure, you have a knowledgeable person to ask, preferably from the firm that set up your plan.

Chapter 6

Real People, Real Stories

I've had the pleasure of speaking to thousands of people over the years about their investment goals with retirement plans. I've learned so much from them. I've also been inspired by them.

There are so many stories I've heard that it's hard to share even a portion of them. However, some stand out. Let me share a few with you. These are real people with real stories – however, I've changed the names for the sake of keeping their privacy.

Beachfront Property

Bob* and Alice* had been looking a long time for a rental opportunity like this: a beautiful beachfront property to rent for a few years, and then move into as a retirement home. The problem was they didn't have enough funds to buy it. Then a friend told them about Self-Directed IRAs. Bob had money in an IRA. Could they really use it to buy this rental?

"Yes," I told them, when they called in. They were ecstatic. With Bob's IRA, they could buy the property outright. They even had a renter lined up. As for moving into it, I told them that as long as the IRA owned the home it was prohibited (see Chapter 5), but when they were ready they could declare the value of the property a distribution, pay the taxes and then move into it. They were doubly ecstatic now!

They signed up and purchased the property within a few weeks.

The Six-Unit Condo

Marcia* and Jose* learned of this six-unit condo in the center of town. They had once heard about Self-Directed IRAs but thought they were expensive and cumbersome to use.

When they called in, I told them the price and that it was as easy to use as using any business account. The difference here was that this LLC bank account (set up at the bank of their choice) was all under the umbrella of a tax-sheltered IRA. They'd use that account to purchase the condo, pay all ongoing maintenance from it and deposit rent checks into it. As long as they did so, their money stayed sheltered from taxes. If they had any questions, legal or technical, they could call us and talk to a knowledgeable representative.

They said they would do their research and get back to me. They did so a few days later, signed up and acquired the condo a couple of weeks after that.

$100,000+ Tax-Sheltered Revenue in a Year

John* from the southeast US, purchased a self-directed IRA with Broad Financial. About a year later, he called to tell me how thrilled he was with the plan and that he had a friend who might be interested in signing up for the same deal.

Then John relayed to me how the plan had worked out for him so far: "…We bought a special little lake place. We have over 450 feet of lakefront. It's beautiful. Great dock. We did that deal. Just now. We did well over $100,000 in revenue last year on a $600,000 investment. And I bought it for a quarter million less than what I can sell it for today. It's a great little success story, if you want to put it on your website.

"I also used the [IRA] LLC for an investment on a foreclosure with a 20% return. Put a caretaker there. He's paying rent. It's not a house I want, so I'm going to let him pay rent for, who knows, 20 years and deed it over to him when he has it all paid back. I'm thrilled with it [the plan] so far."

Avoiding the Next Bubble

Allison* called up inquiring about a plan. During the conversation she explained that, at the time of the last bubble, she and her husband had lost 75% of their retirement savings! It was devastating. They'd worked hard to build it back up.

"The same thing is going to happen again, soon. I see the market. It's the same thing. We want to put our money in real estate. It's the best way to diversify and avoid what happened last time."

Where can you make 20% in an IRA?

Janice* had a question about using a self-directed IRA for real estate. She has been making 20% in her taxable-income real estate deals. There are more deals on the table but she does not have the capital. Then she discovered that she can use her IRA money to invest in real estate – and invest with the same control over her account, not needing to go through a third party for everything (see Chapter 7 about Checkbook IRAs).

During our conversation she remarked, "My IRA is doing nothing in the market. Even when it was doing well, where can I make 20% on an investment? This is an amazing opportunity I never knew about before."

Gold as a Hedge

Prakash* is feeling unsettled about the market. The national debt keeps rising and the government keeps printing more money. This watering down of the US dollar is nothing new, but it's worse than ever, he believes.

Prakash points out that precious metals have protected investors from currency collapses, war, hyperinflation, and even bubbles in the stock, bond and real estate markets. Throughout history, gold and silver have held value in the face of calamity, be it natural or man-made.

Prakash knows a lot about gold and precious metals, but he didn't know until recently that he could use his IRA to buy them. He was thrilled to find out that I confirmed he could indeed do so. Now, however, he had a new question: He had found another firm offering a gold IRA for free! Why did we charge?

I responded that we were not precious metal dealers. We were only offering the *vehicle* to invest in precious metals, *not the metals themselves*. Then I pointed out to him that the reason this other company was offering it for free was because they made their profit in the markup. As long as you purchased the precious metals from them, they were happy to offer a free SD IRA (and that's assuming it was a valid SD IRA).

Prakash signed up.

From New Zealand to Hawaii

Graham* and his wife Lucy* were retired and living in New Zealand. Lucy had worked many years in a US-based Fortune 500 firm and had a nice IRA, but it was languishing in an under-performing mutual fund.

Graham and Lucy had a son living in Hawaii. They wanted to know if it was possible to use Lucy's IRA to buy an investment property her son had identified there. I told them that it was possible by designating their son as the Registered Agent and making him a co-manager of the IRA LLC. That would give him powers to sit at the closing and write a check for the property from the LLC. He would also be able to do all the permitted managerial work (see Chapter 5), such as collecting the rent. The son would deposit the money at the bank and grow Lucy's IRA through its profits.

In essence, the son would be an extension of them, a non-compensated manager of the LLC, never making personal use of the property.

Overseas Real Estate

Fran* had family in Costa Rica. They told her of a wonderful investment property. Fran wanted to know if she could use her IRA to invest in the property. She was thrilled when I told her she could and that we had numerous clients using our plans to invest overseas in real estate.

When she asked how it worked, I told her we set it up the usual way: We create the IRA LLC and send it to her; she takes it to the bank of her choice. The custodian rolls her funds into the bank. At that point, all she will need to do is wire the funds to an LLC in Costa Rica (they required that she set up the equivalent of an LLC there) and acquire the property.

The same rules applied in terms of ongoing maintenance. If money was needed, she'd wire it from the US-based IRA LLC. Once a year, the custodian would work with her to gather the information for the 5498 form (see Chapter 10). If and when she sold it, the profits would flow back to her IRA LLC and stay there tax-deferred until she starting taking distributions (also see Chapter 10).

Realtor Reality

Jane* was a long-time realtor. She had made lots of money over the years as a broker, and as an owner with dozens of rentals. However, she had never heard of SD IRAs and had no idea she could do what she was doing within a tax-sheltered or tax-free (Roth) plan. Then, in a casual conversation, a friend had mentioned the possibility. She researched it and found us.

When I first picked up her call she was still in shock that SD IRAs existed. I assured her that they did and we had thousands of clients using them. Then she told me that she was in a rush. She had identified a rental she was about to purchase and wanted to use her retirement money. The problem was she needed to close in the next day. I explained to her that if she qualified for a Solo 401k (see Chapter 14), it was possible to set it up almost immediately and have the documents to set up the bank account that day or the next. However, the movement of the money from her present account to the 401k account could take more than her time frame.

In the end, her short time frame was not going to work for this rental. However, I explained to her, it sounded ideal for her going forward. She was always on the lookout for new real estate investments, and now with a Self-Directed plan she could do so while receiving tax-sheltered returns. She agreed and even had a couple new possibilities on the horizon. She came on board that day to put herself in position to jump on the next great opportunity.

10x Returns on Ethereum

Henry* contacted us about setting up account to invest in Ethereum, the second-most popular crypto-currency (after bitcoin). We have helped people set up plans to invest in "cryptos" before, but at that time they weren't very popular. Henry wanted to take about $90,000 of IRA funds and invest. No problem. We set it up for him quickly and he opened an account in the name of his IRA LLC at one of the popular cryptocurrency exchanges.

And that was the last I heard of Henry... until about a year later. He told us that his $92,000 had become more than $1 million! All tax-free! (He had he invested with Roth funds.)

Bitcoin Mania

On the topic of bitcoin, we at Broad Financial started getting a noticeable upsurge in calls starting in the spring of 2017. People were not only calling to inquire, but many were in a huge rush to set up a plan and get things started. At that time, I admit that I didn't know much about bitcoin and cryptocurrencies other than that it was a permissible IRA investment. The incredible upsurge in interest led me to begin my own research into the phenomenon. What I discovered was something much bigger than I had imagined, a burgeoning field with wide-ranging applications for the present – including everything from buying pizza to conducting transactions for international shipping operations, for the individual as well as for the largest corporations – and implications for the future. It was a classic example of clients educating me.

Here's a brief list of some of the things I discovered

- A $200 investment in bitcoin is 2011 would be worth over $1 million in 2017!

- Entire countries are using bitcoin as currency.

- It's not just a currency, but a platform for business. Major corporations, including Microsoft, conduct large business transactions using it.

- The technology underlying it is called Blockchain, which is a way to keep records on millions of computers simultaneously, ensuring transparency, increasing the ease of business transactions and reducing the chance of successful hacking.

- Some people see it as a short-term investment, taking advantage of the volatility to their advantage.

- Others see it as a long-term investment, with bitcoin and Ethereum the two leading cryptocurrencies they plan to hold for years to come.

- The state of cryptocurrencies at this stage is so new and so volatile that sound advice is to proceed with caution. Only invest risk capital: money you're willing to lose if it doesn't work out. Diversify into crypto if you wish, but make sure you're not putting all your eggs in one basket.

This represents only a smattering of the ideas I've discovered and that clients have shared with me.

A Crypto IRA Starting with $6,500

Lenny* contacted me several times about setting up an account to invest in various cryptocurrencies. He felt that the best strategy was to put a very small amount – perhaps as low as $100 to $200 – into selected altcoins, as they are called. Altcoins are less-known cryptocurrencies with a high potential for bust but also a high potential to make otherwise-impossible gains. According to Lenny, even if he lost $200 on almost all these altcoins, he would more than make up for it if even one turned into a future cornerstone of the crypto-currency world.

Finally, Lenny called in to set up the plan. After researching which altcoins he wanted to start investing in, he decided to convert his previous year's contributions – $6,500 – into Roth. That way if and when he hit a homerun with one of them his returns would be tax-free.

Lenny's approach shows that it's possible to start with a relatively small amount – money Lenny was willing to lose – for the possibility of enormous tax-free gains, something possible only inside of a self-directed Roth IRA (or Solo 401k).

Crypto Knows No Age

The average age of the crypto IRA investor calling us up is significantly lower than the average age of investors historically: people in their thirties and forties rather than their fifties and sixties. That's no surprise. Cryptocurrency is technology-based and young people have a natural affinity for it. A friend who used to sell software would tell customers, "Our software is so easy even an adult can use it!"

I recently spoke to Al*, a 68-year-old man who had just begun investing in cryptocurrencies and who complained to me that there was a lot to learn from a technological viewpoint. He was having such a hard time figuring out how to move his money from an exchange to a wallet to another exchange and then back to his wallet, etc. that he was thinking about just giving his money to a broker who charged exorbitant fees to do it for him.

After chatting a bit, I was impressed how much Al already knew. Then, I told him that I had just signed up an 88-year-old retired doctor. The doctor's mind was sharp as ever and, although he was fairly new to the cryptocurrency world, he was excited to learn more and more about this new field, and making money in it. I told Al that I didn't think cryptocurrency investing was going to disappear anytime soon; it was only going to grow. If he spent the time learning it, maybe in a couple of years he'd become an expert that people turned to for crypto advice.

At the other end of the spectrum is Leonard. He was 22-years old and had just graduated college. After spending his first three years studying finance, he decided to focus everything on the new world of cryptocurrencies. He became so good at it that friends – and then adults – were paying him $100 per hour to teach them how to invest. Moreover, when Leonard first called me he told me that he was scheduled to make a presentation about cryptocurrency investing at Las Vegas to people paying $10,000 per seat!

The point is that the cryptocurrency world is age-neutral. Young people have a natural proclivity for technology, but older people have invaluable life experience, as well as years of investing experience in many cases. It's a new world open to one and all.

$150,000 Profit Today or Bust!

Frederick* had a very different altcoin strategy. He called up one day in a panic. It was his first call to us. A friend convinced him that a relatively new altcoin was about to shoot up in price in the coming days and if he didn't get in right away he'd lose out on $150,000. He told me he had to get the plan set-up that day so he could make the investment the next day and make that $150,000.

I told him that we could get him set up with a plan, but the only plan that could be set up in that time frame was a Solo 401k (see Chapter 14). Next, I described to him what was needed to qualify for a Solo 401k. He told me that described him.

We got to work right away, signed him up, and emailed him the follow-up paperwork on the spot. (This is only possible with a Solo 401k; a Self-Directed IRA for various reasons cannot be done as quickly.) He filled out the follow-up paperwork while I waited and sent it back. We got his plan set up for him that day.

From that point, I don't know what happened. That's the nature of self-directed checkbook plans. We're creating a vehicle. Once the client takes the vehicle, they can invest without our knowledge. Yes, they can always ask us if what they are doing is within the rules, etc., but we don't necessarily know what they're doing.

Frederick's case shows 1) the incredible potential of cryptocurrencies, 2) the power of a self-directed plan, and 3) the special power of a Solo 401k.

Bitcoin "Flat Rate" IRA

Jeremy* was the first person to sign up with a company that allowed him to invest his IRA money into cryptocurrencies. The fees were high, and they were asset-based. He had to pay them as much as 15% of his investment (e.g. $15,000 on $150,000 investment), and pay them more asset-based fees each time he added money to his account. However, he knew of no other way.

Despite the exorbitant fees he was happy because he was making so much money. In a year's time, he had more than $1 million in his account. The tens of thousands of dollars he paid this company were an annoyance but part of the cost of investing.

Or so he thought. Then he saw that he could move his account to a checkbook IRA at a flat rate for a reasonable amount. No more 15% fees. No more asset-based fees. He called me up to confirm if it was true. It was, I told him. If he moved over a million dollars or added a million dollars he would pay no more than the same flat setup fee and the same flat yearly fee. Jeremy was thrilled and moved his account over.

Investing In Supermodels

Jill* had an unusual way of making money with her retirement money. A friend had approached her with an offer to join an LLC whose value goes up and down based on the 300 or more supermodels it tracks. Truth be told, I didn't really understand how it worked. She said, for instance, that when one of them tweets a product (say a beauty product) it somehow increases the value of the LLC. Whatever the case, Jill wanted to use her IRA money and invest. Could she do it, she asked?

No problem, I told her. She had self-employment income, so we set her up quickly with a Solo 401k. Last I heard from Jill, she was invited to be a judge in a beauty pageant with some of the models.

Arabian Race Horses

Tony spoke with a noticeable New York accent. He wanted to know if he could use his IRA to invest in Arabian race horses. I told him yes and told him about our plan. Along the way he told me about his business and I got a quick primer into the world of thoroughbred racing.

Now, I don't pretend to know anything about horses, to say nothing of thoroughbreds, but Tony proceeded to tell me a lot about them. First, he was inspired by American Pharaoh, who had recently entered thoroughbred racing's all-time greats by winning the Belmont Stakes to become the first horse to capture the coveted Triple Crown in nearly four decades.

Tony told me about some of the costs and the risks involved of investing in Arabian race horses. You bought the horse when it was very young. You made sure it was the offspring of a real thoroughbred. You then spent the next few years paying all the costs to raise it, including special food, a highly-regarded trainer, etc. It was a lot of money, he kept reassuring me. Then, and only then would you find out if it was a winner. Often, they're not, he said. But if they are, you make an enormous profit, besides all the publicity.

Chapter 7

The 2 Types of SD IRAs: Custodial & Checkbook

Often people call up confused about the cost to establish an SD IRA. They've done some shopping and they find that pricing can vary greatly. Setup costs can be as low as $100 and as high as $2,000 or more. Why the discrepancy?

What they don't know is that there are two fundamentally different types of SD IRAs: custodial and checkbook. Each works differently and, depending upon your investment choices, one might be better for you than the other.

Custodial SD IRAs

A custodial SD IRA means that your money is held at a third party's bank account; a custodian. When you need a check – whether a big one to purchase a property or a small one to pay a small utility bill – you must request it from the custodian. Someone there processes the request and sends the check out on your behalf.

Custodian's typically charge a small setup fee. They make their money in asset-based fees or transaction feels. Or some combination thereof.

Checkbook IRAs

A checkbook IRA allows you to put your IRA money fully in your hands. Through the creation of a specialized LLC – often called an

"IRA LLC" – you can open an LLC account at your local bank. Then a custodian will roll your money from where it is into that bank where your new IRA LLC is.

Every IRA needs a custodian, but in a checkbook plan, the custodian is "passive." Their main function is not to *hold* your money but to *move* it. Once it's moved, they have no control over it. Only you do.

So Which Is Better?

In short, the more check-intensive your investment, the more a checkbook plan makes sense.

Real estate rentals, for example, are check-intensive. You need checks every month to pay for costs like utility bills, repairs, landscaping, property taxes, etc. Even if you need as little as two or three checks a month, the checkbook plan will probably prove more cost-effective when you crunch the numbers.

However, that's not the only advantage of a checkbook plan. Just as important is the instant, unfettered access to your funds. You don't have to contact a custodian to get them. Even with a competent, organized custodian (and not all of them are; see the next chapter) there is a time lag between requesting a check and getting your money. Sometimes, it gets lost or they don't send it to the right address or in the right amount or sometimes they're simply late despite all the advanced notice you give them. That can lead to late fees or worse: losing out on a deal. I've had people call me who lost deals because the custodian's check came too late.

On the other hand, some people are not planning on managing an IRA-property. All they need is the ability to send one check to fund an LLC, business or the like. Periodically, they will receive dividends or returns, but they are not involved in a check-intensive investment. In such a case, they are typically better served by a custodial plan. There's a small, one-time setup fee (often including the first check) and a fixed yearly service fee (unless the custodian charges an asset-based fee), and that's all they pay.

Ideally, you want to talk to a company that offers both a custodial option and a genuine checkbook option. A one-dimensional company might try to sell you their plan even though it is not the best thing for you. Ask if they offer both.

One last thing to be aware of is that some custodial companies try to mask the fact that they're a custodian by creating what seems like a hybrid of the custodial and checkbook model. For instance, they may provide some sort of online portal to write checks from, as if the money was at your local bank. Buyer beware. It's possible that this setup can work for some people, but you may be paying more because they are basing their charges on asset-based fees and/or transaction fees.

In a true checkbook plan, your money is at a bank of your choice. You don't need to go through anyone or any portal run by the custodian. They are not holding or controlling your assets in any way. Therefore, there are no asset-based or transaction fees. Most important of all, you have instant access to your money.

Once again, crunch the numbers and do your own research. The fixed low-cost service fees and full control of your money in a checkbook plan are probably a better bet for check-intensive investments like real estate.

Chapter 8

Beware of Scams, Fly-By-Nights, Pajama Salesmen & Bad Customer Service

Manufacturer Sy Syms made famous the slogan: "An educated consumer is our best customer." So true – especially in the realm of SD IRAs. Basically, you want to be on the lookout for scams, fly-by-nights and bad customer service.

Scams

A person calls us and says that they signed up for an SD IRA with checkbook control but they can't get through to the company. They want to know if we can adopt their plan. I tell them that they can email me their LLC and I'll show it to our compliance department. More than once it's happened that the LLC was invalid. In other words, they were given a plan put together by amateurs, jeopardizing the tax-sheltered status of their IRA money. They were scammed.

Sometimes, it's not necessarily a scammer, but they trusted their attorney to write up a proper IRA LLC; one that can hold retirement money. But the attorney did not know what he was doing. "But he's a tax attorney," the caller tells me.

"Tax attorneys don't necessarily know about retirement law," I respond. "What you need is an ERISA attorney or at least an attorney that knows the basics of ERISA law." (ERISA stands for "Employee Retirement Income Security Act," which was established in 1974 by the federal government to set minimum standards for pensions and retirement plans in private industry to protect individuals in these plans. It's a very specialized field within law.)

A similar situation is a person who calls up and says they set up their own LLC – a "homemade" LLC based on their understanding of the law. They did not realize that an IRA LLC is *not* a regular LLC. Regular LLCs can't hold retirement monies and can't use those monies to purchase real estate or the like. A proper IRA LLC has been crafted by ERISA attorneys to conform with IRS retirement law.

Fly-By-Nights & Pajama Salesmen

The next type of buyer-beware situation is what I call "fly-by-nights." These are companies offering SD IRAs that have sprung up recently and have no track record. They advertise extremely low prices. As the saying goes: If it's too good to be true... it often is.

A woman called me up and said she had found someone offering an SD IRA but for considerably less. I asked her the name of the company. She told me the name. I had never heard of it (which is unusual, because there aren't a whole lot of players out there). I did a quick Google search as we spoke and found the company's address. Then I went to Google Maps and zoomed in. It was a house in a residential area.

I told the woman to Google the address and zoom in on it herself. She did. She then realized that it was a house. I said, "It sounds to me like you've got a guy in his basement trying to sell you a Self-Directed IRA."

Of course, anything is possible. But, generally, you want a) an established company and b) you want... a company. You don't want Al who works from home in his pajamas. Now, Al may be a nice guy. He may even be a guy with a legal background. But in a year from now Al might get bored or find something else to do with his life. As I said, I've had people call me up and say that they can't get through to the people who sold them the original plan. They have questions. There are IRS reports to complete. They're helpless. But Al has flown the coop.

That's the problem with a fly-by-night. It's your retirement. Don't save a few dollars only to find out later that your hard-saved retirement money may be in jeopardy of losing its tax-sheltered status.

Bad Customer Service

The third thing to watch out for is bad customer service. You've determined that you're dealing with a real company; one that has more than one or two employees. They have a sales division, a processing division, a customer service division, an IT department, an executive board, etc. They even have a track record. They're more than a few years old.

I always tell people that you're not only looking for a *plan*, but a *company*. If you thought you had questions before you started, chances are you'll have even more questions after you start; real questions. Who do you turn to if you have questions? That's why you need a company to support you going forward. It's arguably the most important part of your decision-making process.

You need a company with customer service people who are a) knowledgeable and b) available. And you need to do your research to make sure they have a track record to do it. The Better Business Bureau (BBB) is a good place to start.

Unfortunately, one of the larger, longer-running, more visible custodial companies also has the worst reputation for customer service. I won't mention it by name (let's refer to them as "Company X"), but I know this firsthand, because every week we get calls from some of their disgruntled customers. (I call them "refugees" from Company X.)

Sometimes, a person calls in and tells me they are fed up with the custodian they've been with. Before they tell me the name of the custodian, I often ask "Is it Company X?"

"Yes," they say with wonder. "How did you know?"

I'm not clairvoyant, I tell them. I just have a lot of experience.

If people ask, I will sometimes point them to a *Wall Street Journal* article which names Company X as the target of a class-action lawsuit for misappropriation of funds. (Note: the potential for misappropriation of funds only exists in a custodial plan, because the custodian holds the funds. In a checkbook plan, your funds are in your hands at a local bank you choose, not at a custodian.)

To be fair, it's not always that company. There are others that have bad reputations. But it's sad how often people complain about this company. Also, to be fair, I assume they have happy customers too. The calls we receive are from the unhappy ones.

Whoever it is, the complaints against bad companies are predictable: You can't get through to anyone there. They never return calls. When you talk to them, customer service is terrible.

Sometimes, the service is so terrible that the caller loses out on a deal. In short, they had a deadline to buy a property, but the custodian took their time approving the deal.

The bottom line is that, at least as important as the plan you choose (whether it's custodial or checkbook), is the company you choose. A good company can give you peace of mind that's priceless, and help you steer clear of any potential issues. A bad company can make a fairly simple process nightmarish.

Chapter 9

Roths, Trads, SEPs and Simples

Just as brokerage-based IRAs can come in several flavors, so too Self-Directed IRAs. You have Traditional, Roth and SEPs. (You can also open a Simple IRA, but these are less and less common and, in Orwellian fashion, are not so simple...)

Traditional SD IRA

This is the bread-and-butter of the entire retirement industry. Most people have them. In a traditional IRA, your money is tax-deferred. It's not tax-free. You're going to pay taxes on it one day. But not until you retire or voluntarily take a distribution (a distribution means you're telling the IRS you want to use your money personally and you're willing to pay the taxes on the amount you take out or "distribute").

A common question people ask is: Can they pay themselves a salary for some type of payment for services? The answer is no. You can't give yourself a salary. But you can take a distribution, which means filling out a form available through your custodian, who lets the IRS know that you want to take a distribution. You can then use that money personally. That's not a salary; it's a distribution. The IRA is designed for the profits to flow back into the IRA and from there build up until you retire. But you can always take out what you want before. You just pay the taxes.

Regular IRAs and SD IRAs are subject to the same basic rules. Therefore, if you take a distribution before age 59½, you will also pay a 10% penalty. The rules of RMDs ("Required Minimum Distributions") are the same too. At 70½, you must start drawing RMDs. The amount is based on actuarial tables and other factors, so you will need an accountant or the like to tell you how much you're required to distribute.

You can also make contributions into an SD IRA just like a regular IRA.

A common question unique to SD IRAs is whether an asset, like property, can be taken as a distribution. Say you have a $100,000 property, which you purchased with your IRA. You've had it for years and it earned a nice return through rentals. Now, you or your spouse are retiring and you'd like to live in it. As you know from above, it would be prohibited for you to live in an IRA-owned house. However, you can take its value as a distribution, pay the taxes on it and then live in it.

Roth

Just as traditional IRAs work by the same basic rules, whether they are brokerage-based or self-directed, so too Roth IRAs.

A Roth IRA is when you pay the taxes up front. You pay now rather than later. What's the advantage to that? Well, besides the fact that the government likes to be paid sooner rather than later, there's a significant advantage. Roth money is not just tax-*deferred*. It's tax-*free*. More importantly, not only does your *principal* in a Roth investment come back tax-free, but so does your *profit*!

Remember the doctor I mentioned above who wanted to invest $125,000 in a startup pharmaceutical company? Well, he told me that, if it succeeded like he thought, it could relatively quickly turn his investment into $2 million. If he did that with a traditional SD IRA, he would not have to pay taxes on it until he retired. But, his $125,000 was Roth money. He had paid the taxes long ago. He was hoping to not only get his $125,000 returned tax-free, but his entire profit!

In truth, his pharmaceutical start-up would probably be considered an active business, meaning that his profit would be subject to UBIT (see next chapter), which is a special tax on profits even though the money is in an IRA – and even if the money is Roth. However, for argument's sake, say he was investing in a non-UBIT-triggering startup (e.g. rental). If so, he would get the full $2 million tax free!

Now, between you and me, I'd be ecstatic with even a *tax-deferred* gain like that. Okay, eventually I'd have to pay taxes on the $2 million. Let's even say it was some exorbitant percentage like 40%. I'd figure how to squeeze by on the remaining $1.2 million. But this doctor had a better plan (at least, he thought he did). If his idea worked he'd have the full $2 million to live off without paying any more taxes!

That's the power of a Roth account. Combined with an SD IRA and a great investment, it's an amazing way to invest. (By the way, I never found out if his pharmaceutical startup hit pay dirt as he hoped.)

One last note, unlike a traditional IRA, there are no RMDs with a Roth IRA at 70½. You never have to take out the money if you don't want to. And if you do take it out, it's tax-free.

Keep in mind that converting your retirement money to Roth is not for everyone. Often people can't afford to do it now. In all cases, consult with your accountant.

SEP

SEP stands for Simplified Employee Pension. It's for self-employed people (also with the initials SEP). A SEP-IRA account is a traditional IRA and follows the same investment, distribution, and rollover rules as traditional IRAs.

Check the rules on the IRS website (https://www.irs.gov/retirement-plans/retirement-plans-faqs-regarding-seps), especially as it relates to your employees. If you are self-employed but have no full-time employees, then you should consider a Solo 401k.

One of the advantages of a SEP over a traditional IRA is that it has a much higher contribution ceiling. Almost ten times as much!

Chapter 10

Taxes, Reporting and UBIT

A common question is: In an SD IRA, who does my taxes? The custodian?

The good news is: There are no taxes! That's why it's an IRA. You don't pay taxes on it!

Unless, of course, you voluntarily take a distribution or you reach 70½. In those cases, you'll fill out paperwork at the custodian that you're taking a distribution from. They will alert the IRS. It will trigger a form called a 1099R. Based on the 1099R, you will pay your taxes to the IRS.

In most cases though, most people will not take distributions. They'll keep their money in investments and let them grow without paying taxes until they retire or hit 70½.

What about reporting? Is there any reporting required?

Yes, it's called form 5498. The 5498 is not a tax form, however. It's a "valuation" form. The IRS wants to know the *value* of your assets from year to year. When you add up the cash and the value of, say, your properties, what does it equal; what's its value?

It's the custodian's responsibility to reach out to you to collect the information. They will process it and submit it to the IRS.

Some people say: It can't be that easy! No tax reporting and a simple, generic valuation form? But that's all they want. Of course, you must keep a precise paper trail of all your transactions in case you're ever audited. If you're audited, you will have to show them all the payables and all the receivables. Everything. Many clients use a program like Quickbooks to track it. Whatever you use, you'll keep internal records just like any business or real estate endeavor. You may never need to show this paperwork to the IRS. In fact, you probably won't. Statistically, only a small percent of people get audited. However, you don't want to be caught without a paper trail if you are. If you've been diligent in keeping the proper records you should have nothing to worry about.

On the subject of audits, people often ask if a self-directed plan increases the chance of an audit. It does not. More on that later.

UBIT? You Bet

The last thing to know in this section is something called UBIT, which stands for "Unrelated Business Income Tax" (sometimes it's referred to as UBTI). It's a tax that applies even in an IRA. You trigger it if you use your IRA in a way that the IRS deems is an "active business."

What's an active business? For example, the operation of a gas station, dry cleaner, grocery store, etc. If your IRA invests in it, then the net profit of the business would be subject to UBIT.

The more common investments, such as real estate, tax-liens, mortgages, securities, etc., are typically exempt from UBIT. In fact, most investors never run into it, because the types of investments favored by the self-directed platform are normally passive in nature.

One common UBIT question arises for people who "flip" properties. Although real estate rentals are normally considered passive investments, if an investor engages in active property-flipping, it could trigger UBIT.

How would you know if your property transactions are considered active or passive?

The generally accepted distinction is that properties that are sold after they are held for a year or longer are not considered "flipped." Those held for less than a year and then sold might be considered "flipped."

I say "might be" because there's a gray area here. The IRS code uses the word "frequent." What's frequent? Well, one flip a year is not frequent. A person can say that they purchased the property with the intention to hold, but then they were given an offer they couldn't refuse. If that happened once in a year, it's plausible. An occasional flip will not trigger UBIT.

However, more than once in a twelve-month period can already trigger UBIT. Some people believe they can flip three or four per year without UBIT. In all cases of uncertainty, ask an ERISA attorney for the details of your specific case.

How much is UBIT?

It's a tiered-tax on the profits. It goes up the more profit you make until it maxes out at 39.6%. As an example, say you buy a house for $100,000 and flip it for $150,000. If that's the only flip you do within a 12-month period, you are fine. No UBIT. But the second one might trigger UBIT. If it is, of that $50,000 profit you may owe the IRS about $20,000.

Despite that, I've had people tell me it's still worth it to them, because they make so much money. Either way, it's important to be aware of UBIT and have knowledgeable people to discuss if it applies in your case.

Chapter 11

Loans, Leverage and Lenders

A common question runs something along the following lines: "I don't have enough money to purchase the house outright. Only enough for a down payment. Can I get a loan?"

The answer is yes, but it can only be a non-recourse loan.

Most loans given by banks and financial institutions are "recourse" loans. They, the lender, have recourse to your personal assets should you default on the loan. The bank may not consider the property you're purchasing with the loan enough as collateral. They want you to have more "skin in the game."

In a non-recourse loan, the lender has no recourse to your personal assets. That means most banks won't offer it. It means that using IRA money for a down payment and hoping to get a loan on the rest is not as easy as a non-IRA property. Most of our clients are purchasing their properties outright (or co-investing; see next chapter).

Nevertheless, it is doable and I've had several clients happily investing their IRAs with non-recourse loans. I remember one young entrepreneur who had the opportunity to buy a multi-dweller home in a university neighborhood where the students rented. She told me that the great thing about renting to university students is that they never missed their payments – their wealthy parents, that is, never missed their payments. It was a slam dunk for her.

The problem was that she only had enough money in her IRA for a down payment of 50%. I told her that she needed a non-recourse loan. We connected her to a non-recourse lender who had success with previous clients. She was approved and purchased the home.

She called me a few months later to tell me how she was happy with the whole arrangement. It was such an amazing deal, in fact, that she liquidated other IRA money to buy a second home in the same university neighborhood with the same non-recourse lender.

It was great for me to learn it worked out well for her. Not enough people contact me and tell me how happy they are. But she did, and I'm grateful to her. However, I would be remiss if I did not reiterate once again that getting a non-recourse loan can be challenging.

As an aside, other than non-recourse banks, other ways of acquiring non-recourse loans include cutting a deal with the seller. Sometimes, they want to sell so much that they're happy to supply seller financing through a non-recourse loan. Just make sure you have language in the contract to indicate that it's a non-recourse loan (i.e. no personal guarantee).

Another potential source of non-recourse loans is a person with an SD IRA! Some of our most successful clients, as I said, are using the plan to make bridge loans or the like.

As with all such investments, do your due diligence.

UDFI

Another challenge with non-recourse loans is UDFI, "Unrelated Debt Finance Income." UDFI is a subset of UBIT (see previous chapter). The loan portion of the deal is subject to UDFI, which is a tax on the profits from the leveraged portion.

For example, if an IRA's LLC purchases a property and funds the purchase 60% with its own money and 40% from borrowed money, then, in general, 40% of the IRA's share of net profits will be subject to UDFI, because that portion of the profits was created from money that was not owned by the IRA's LLC.

Here's a practical example:

Let's say you have $50,000 in your IRA. You shop around for potential investments and you find a property for $150,000. To facilitate the purchase, you have your IRA borrow $100,000. Your IRA then purchases the property. A year later you find a buyer for the property. The sale price is $240,000. That means that your IRA just netted $90,000 on the deal. However, not all that profit is due to tax-deferred IRA funds. Only one-third of it can be attributed to the IRA. The other two-thirds is attributed to the loan that the IRA took out to purchase the property. Then, as it does every year, tax time rolls around. The $30,000 profit that came from the IRA is tax deferred. The $60,000 that came from the loan has to pay UDFI and the remainder goes back in tax-deferred.

Note: For real estate transactions, a Solo 401k is exempt from UDFI. We discuss that in our Solo 401k Guide.

Chapter 12

Investing, Co-Investing, Co-mingling

In the previous chapter, we mentioned that one way to purchase a property that your IRA does not have enough money to buy outright is to get a non-recourse loan. Another way is "co-investing."

Co-investing means going into a deal at the outset with partners. Say there is a house worth $100,000, but your IRA only has $50,000. You can find a partner and co-invest with them. Perfectly legitimate. So much so, in fact, that you can even co-invest with an otherwise disqualified person (see Chapter 5). You can even co-invest with yourself!

For example, you take $50,000 from your IRA and $50,000 from your regular, taxable bank account. You can co-invest them to purchase that $100,000 property. You just should be aware that, in that case, 50% of your returns will go back into the IRA and are tax-sheltered, and 50% goes back to you personally and are taxable.

If you want to co-invest, you might want to consider creating a "sub-LLC," which is a regular LLC that will have two (or more) members. Say, for example, a husband and wife want to co-invest their IRAs into an investment property. The "sub-LLC" will have as members her SD IRA and his SD IRA. This "sub-LLC" will acquire title to the property. All expenses will be paid from the "sub-LLC" and all rent will be deposited into the sub-LLC account. The advantage of this is that you only have to write one check for expenses, and your renters only have to write one check to the "sub-LLC." Otherwise, the husband and wife would have to write two proportional checks for every expense, and their renters would have to write two checks: one to her SD IRA and one to his.

Co-investing is sometimes confused with co-mingling. You can co-invest but you can't co-mingle. Co-investing is, as we said, when you structure a deal from the *beginning* with other partners, be they disqualified or not. Co-mingling means you've already purchased, say, raw land, with regular, taxable money. Now you want to use your IRA to build on it. You can't. That would be co-mingling. Once a property is purchased with personal funds it can't be co-mingled with IRA funds.

Similarly, if you have set up a checkbook plan, i.e. an IRA LLC, you can only put IRA funds in it. You can't co-mingle personal funds into it. The two must be kept separate.

Chapter 13

Yeah, But Is It Legal?

It would be terrible if I made you read all this up to now and I then told you it's illegal.

The good news is that SD IRAs are perfectly legal and have been in circulation for decades. Nevertheless, I'm not insulted when people ask me for an opinion letter from our ERISA attorneys on the subject. I gladly email it to them.

A funny story happened to me a few years ago, when I got a call from a Harvard professor of Economics. He asked me if I could produce an opinion letter for him. I told him I'd email it to him. A day or two later, he emailed me back and added more sources to buttress the argument. Here's what he wrote:

> Thank you, Jeff. The opinion letter is very helpful. Also helpful, for your information, is what Wikipedia says (in their entry on self-directed IRAs) about LLCs:

> Although Swanson v. Commissioner doesn't directly relate to a single member IRA LLC, but instead merely sets a precedent that an individual can manage and control an entity owned by an IRA or IRAs that they are a disqualified person to, there are other cases, private letter rulings and IRS Memorandums that corroborate the validity of using retirement funds to invest in a special purpose entity, such as an LLC, wholly owned by an IRA. The recent Tax Court case Peek v. Commissioner, 140 T.C.

No. 12 (May 9, 2013) reinforced the ability for a retirement account investor to use retirement funds to invest in a wholly owned entity without triggering a prohibited transaction. In the Peek case, the U.S. Tax Court ruled that a taxpayer's personal guaranty of a loan by a corporation owned by the individual's IRA is a prohibited transaction under section 4975(c)(1)(B). The Tax Court found that the taxpayers had provided an indirect extension of credit to the IRAs, a prohibited transaction under Internal Revenue Code Section 4975 that disqualified the IRAs. The Tax Court did not, however, have an issue with the taxpayer forming a special purpose corporation to make the investment as well as serve as director and registered agent of the corporation.

For more information on IRA LLC law see:

- *U.S. Code Title 26 Section 408 and 4975*

- *Ancira v. Commissioner 119 T.C. No. 6 (2002) – Ancira acted as a conduit for her self-directed IRA custodian*

- *Swanson v. Commissioner 106 t.c. 76 (1996) – Swanson directed his IRA to invest in a company which he controlled and was also owned by the IRAs of his 3 children*

- *DOL Advisory Opinions 97-23A and 2005-03A – The Department of Labor takes the position that if an asset is owned 100% by a plan, that asset becomes the plan*

- *IRS Field Service Advice 200128011 – IRS Confirms: "The type of investment that may be held in an IRA is limited only with respect to insurance contracts, under section 408(a)(3), and with respect to certain collectibles, under section 408(m)(1)"*

- *Peek v. Commissioner, 140 T.C. No. 12 (May 9, 2013) – a taxpayer's personal guaranty of a loan by a corporation owned by the individual's IRA is a prohibited transaction under section 4975(c)(1)(B).*

I include the professor's addendum now whenever someone asks me for an opinion letter.

Having said that, I would be remiss if I didn't tell you that I get calls from people who say they have seen claims on the internet that the IRS doesn't favor checkbook plans. Have I heard of such issues?

First, I tell them that there is a lot of misinformation out there, some of it peddled by companies with a vested interest in sowing doubt in checkbook plans, which they see as competition. (That's one reason why it's advantageous to find a company that offers both a custodial plan and a checkbook plan, so you are not talking to someone with a vested interest in only one type of plan.)

Some of the confusion is ignorance. ERISA law is complicated. Even otherwise knowledgeable attorneys and accountants may be unaware of ERISA law as it relates to self-directed IRAs. Note: ERISA attorneys specialize in retirement law. They should typically be the first ones to ask about self-directed IRAs/401ks, even before tax attorneys. Therefore, an important question is: Is the information from an ERISA attorney or from somewhere else?

In either event, it can happen that otherwise knowledgeable financial people pick up on the misinformation and pass it along without really knowing about checkbook plans. When people ask me for the legal basis, I happily offer to send them the opinion letter, with the addendums of the Harvard professor.

Six Relevant Lawsuits

Either way, for those with a legal background here are six relevant lawsuits, and what we learn from each of them:

Swanson (1996) – The Tax Court ruled in favor of Mr. Swanson that an IRA is allowed to invest into a newly formed entity (e.g. corporation, LLC).

Pentegra (1997) – Once an IRA invests into and owns the LLC, then all future transactions between the IRA and the IRA LLC are considered intra-plan transactions (and not transactions between the Plan/IRA and a party in interest, which could be construed as a Prohibited Transaction). In other words, you can add additional retirement funds into the plan.

Hellweg (2011) – Similar to Swanson, the Tax Court ruled in favor of Mr. Hellweg that an IRA (specifically in his case, a Roth IRA) can invest/purchase 100% ownership of a newly formed entity (e.g. corporation, LLC).

Ellis (2013) – Same deal as Hellweg, however, the Tax Court held that Mr. Ellis did engage in a Prohibited Transaction when he caused his IRA LLC to compensate him for managing the IRA LLC.

Rollins (2004) – If an IRA transacts with an entity in which a Disqualified Person has an ownership interest of less than 50% (so that the entity is not disqualified), the transaction still needs to be scrutinized for potential Prohibited Transactions.

Bobrow (2014) – You can only perform one indirect IRA rollover per 12-month period (this is a serious departure from the old 1981 IRS ruling, as stated in Publication 590, that you can perform one indirect rollover per IRA per 12-month period). [Please note: The one per year rule only applies to *indirect_rollovers*. This means that if you take a *taxable, personal* distribution from one IRA, you are permitted to deposit the distribution into a different IRA within 60-days and you won't be taxed on the distribution. This can only be done once a year. *Direct* transfers (moving funds directly from one IRA custodian to another), can be done as many times as you want.]

Chapter 14

The Self-Directed Solo 401k

A Self-Directed Solo 401k is very much like a Self-Directed IRA in that both afford you "checkbook control" (i.e., the ability to perform your own transactions). You can take your retirement money, put it in a bank of your choice and from there, invest it as you would into any permitted asset such as real estate, bitcoin/cryptocurrencies, loans, tax liens, precious metals, etc.

With a Solo 401k, you can do everything you can do with an SD IRA; in addition, it has a lot of other advantages. Before the advantages though, let's mention a couple of disadvantages.

One is that, unlike an IRA where everyone qualifies, the Solo 401k does have eligibility requirements: you need self-employment income ("active" self-employment – more on that ahead), but can have no full-time employees working for you. The self-employment income can originate from your LLC, corporation, or you can be a sole proprietor, meaning somebody making money from 1099-work, e.g. consulting and being paid in a check made out to you personally.

The minimum amount that you need to make as a self-employed person is $500 per year (net profit). The other qualification is that you cannot have full-time employees, meaning non-related W2 employees who work 1,000 hours or more per year. A thousand hours per year would be about 20 hours a week, times 50 weeks. Even one such employee in even one of perhaps several businesses would disqualify you from a Solo 401k (but it's always best to speak to a professional if you are seeking to establish a Solo 401k).

If you have sub-contractors, for instance, being paid on a 1099, they don't disqualify you. If they are being paid on a W-2 by you, but they work less than 1,000 hours per year, they don't disqualify you. If you meet the qualifications, you can start a Solo 401k. If you don't, you still have the power and control of the Self-Directed IRA option.

The only other significant potential disadvantage to the Solo 401k vs. the SD IRA is if you have *existing* Roth IRA money or an Inherited IRA, and you want to roll it into a new Self-Directed plan; you can't do so in a Solo 401k. Traditional IRA money can be rolled into a Solo 401k. Roth 401k can be rolled into a Solo 401k, just not an existing Roth IRA. However, if you have *Traditional* IRA money you can roll it into your Solo 401k and then *convert* it into Roth once it's in the Solo 401k because the Solo 401k plan has a Roth component.

Those are the two basic disadvantages. You must qualify with self-employment income and you can't use Roth IRA money.

Now, onto the advantages.

First, the solo 401k costs less to set up and maintain.

Second, the contribution ceiling is much higher. In an IRA, if you're under 50, for instance, you can contribute $5,500 per year. If you're 50 or over, it's $6500 per year (whether a Roth or Traditional). In a solo 401k, it's almost 10 times that! If you're under 50 years of age, it's $54,000 per year and if you're 50 or over, it's $60,000 per year! So, you have a much higher contribution ceiling with a Solo 401k.

Third, there's no custodian. In an SD IRA, you need a custodian, a middle party to roll your money over. You also need the custodian to take care of the yearly required IRS form (the 5498). If you're going to make contributions or take distributions, you need to go through the custodian. Typically, a custodian will add a couple of days to the process as well as costs. In a Solo 401k, there's no custodian. You are your own plan administrator. If you want to roll funds over, you simply contact the institution holding your funds. This can save time and money.

The same thing with any contributions or distributions: you do it, not a custodian. There will be no fees involved and no middle party to work through.

Fourth, in an SD IRA, the legal entity that holds the money is an LLC. In a 401k, it's a trust. LLCs typically have additional costs involved in the set-up and maintenance. LLCs are regulated by each state and most states charge a yearly fee to keep the LLC going. Some states like California charge $800 per year for an LLC. Most charge under $100 per year, and some charge nothing.

Fifth, a major advantage of the Solo 401k is the personal loan feature. In an IRA, you could make loans to *others*, but you can't take money out as a personal loan to yourself. In a Solo, however, you can also take a personal loan, which means a loan where you can use the money for whatever you want: to invest in your own business, to pay off a mortgage or credit card, to take a vacation. You just have to pay it back. You have five years to pay it back. You pay it back quarterly and you pay it back with a little bit of interest to yourself.

How much are you allowed as a personal loan in the Solo 401k? Up to 50% of your account, capped off at $50,000. Say, for instance, you have $60,000 in your Solo 401k. You can take a personal loan of up to $30,000. If you have $100,000 or more, you can max out the $50,000 loan.

The sixth advantage is the Roth component. In an SD IRA, Roth and Traditional money must be in their own plans; you will need two IRAs if you want to use both: one SD IRA for the Roth and one for the Traditional money. The Solo 401k can simultaneously hold both types of money: you can have Roth and you can have Traditional in the one plan without having to pay twice.

A seventh advantage is that it is relatively easy for a husband and wife to share a Solo 401k. In an IRA, if a husband and wife each have their own IRAs, they typically need to pay for two SD IRA plans. His IRA can't be rolled into her IRA, and vice versa. However, when a husband and wife are partners on an LLC or S-Corp, for instance, they need only one Solo 401k plan. Seek out a professional to confirm if you and your spouse can share a Solo 401k.

There are other advantages, but one final advantage to note is that the Solo 401k is a lot faster to set up. Without expediting it can take a week or two. With expediting a day or two; in some cases, the same day! By contrast, the typical SD IRA setup takes two to three weeks (although potentially faster with expediting).

In short, the Solo 401k is a superior product... if you qualify. If not, the SD IRA is still a fantastic vehicle. Many people have built up bigger and more secure retirement portfolios with both types of plans.

Chapter 15

Rapid-Fire Q & A

These are some of the common questions people have, presently here in no particular order.

Just starting out

Question: I'm just starting out. I don't have any retirement money saved. Can I start a Self-Directed IRA?

Answer: You can, but you don't need to now. Until you have enough money to invest in alternative assets, it's probably a better idea to open an IRA at your bank or at an online brokerage. Bank and brokerage IRAs are often free. SD IRAs are not free. They require specialized expertise to set up, and that expertise comes along with a cost – a modest cost, but a cost nonetheless. Therefore, if you're just starting out, open a free IRA and build it up. (Note: If you're self-employed, you can build your retirement pot up *almost ten times faster* with a SEP IRA or Solo 401k.)

Can I roll over my company plan?

Question: Can I roll over a 401k from my current employer?

Answer: Probably not, but it depends on your company. As long as you work there, they have the right to keep your retirement funds locked up in their plan. Once you no longer work there, you have the rights: they can't force you to keep your retirement with them.

Don't assume they're locked up. Especially if you have been there many years and/or have reached a certain age. There should be someone at your company to ask; probably someone with the title, "Plan Administrator" or the like.

Risky?

Question: Is a self-directed plan inherently risky?

Answer: Sometimes, I get calls from people saying that the checkbook control platform is too risky, claiming that it's too easy to perform a prohibited transaction. The truth is that, with the proper education, the chance of committing a prohibited transaction is virtually zero. Make sure you sign up with a company that has the reputation of supplying excellent educational material, and an impeccable record for customer service so you can get answers to any questions you may have.

Isn't a custodial plan safer?

Question: Isn't a custodial plan safer than a checkbook plan?

Answer: A man with a custodial SD IRA called in and, after talking to him, we found out that he was unaware that his transactions were subject to UBIT (he was flipping houses on a regular basis; see Chapter 10), which meant that he owed a special tax on his IRA profits. The custodian never informed him. And he had been with them for ten years!

Another caller got fed up with his custodian after he got a call from the municipality where he had purchased a property with his IRA. The call was to inform him that his property was about to go into foreclosure for failure to pay a certain annual fee. The custodian was supposed to pay that fee, but never did, and this caller only found out after the property was about to be foreclosed.

In the custodial model, people are sometimes lulled into a false sense of security, believing that everything is being taken care of, and being taken care of competently. They tend to become passive about knowing the rules.

In a checkbook plan, it's up to you. And once you know that the burden is on you, you do everything you can on your own and take advantage of the customer service people of the checkbook company you signed up with either a) as a backup to confirm what you understand and/or b) as a resource to ask them to tell you what you don't know.

Attorneys on Staff

Question: Is it necessary for the company I sign up with to have attorneys on staff?

Answer: They must have attorneys – specifically ERISA attorneys – on retainer, but not necessarily on staff. Attorneys are expensive, and ERISA attorneys tend to be even more so. Any competent company has relied upon them to set up their plans and should still have access to them should a client ask a particularly knotty question. However, most clients ask questions that a properly-trained customer service rep can answer on the spot. Such customer service people need higher-ups, but don't necessarily need to be expensive ERISA attorneys. In fact, oftentimes firms that advertise attorneys on staff are *not* ERISA attorneys anyway!

One of the early players in the SD IRA field (when I began five years ago), dropped out because their prices were eventually not competitive, and they couldn't bring them down because they had attorneys on staff. You need a reputable company with well-trained customer service representatives who, if need be, have access to the most knowledgeable people (their knowledge passed onto you at no additional cost).

Taxed or penalized for rollovers?

Question: Will I be taxed or penalized if I roll over money into a Self-Directed IRA?

Answer: No. Rollovers/transfers are non-taxable events. If you roll over your existing IRA into a Self-Directed IRA, there will be no taxes or penalties. It's a *direct* transfer; the funds are never titled in your personal name, only in the name of the IRA.

Who owns the LLC?

Question: Who owns the LLC in a checkbook IRA?

Answer: The IRA. In short, it works like this: The custodian sets up the IRA. The facilitator sets up the LLC. The IRA owns the LLC. The IRA holder – you! – becomes the non-compensated manager. This means that you can conduct all the business of the LLC, but you are not compensated for it. Because the LLC is owned by the Self-Directed IRA, the assets you purchase are also, then, owned by your SD IRA. They become part of your retirement portfolio.

Can I use my own LLC?

Question: I have my own LLC; can I use it to put IRA funds into?

Answer: An IRA LLC is not a regular LLC. Regular LLCs can't hold retirement monies and can't use those monies to purchase real estate or the like. A proper IRA LLC has been crafted by ERISA attorneys to conform with IRS retirement law. So, unless your LLC has been crafted in conformity with ERISA law, it will not be allowed to receive retirement cash and assets.

What types of retirement money can be rolled over?

Question: What type of retirement funds can be rolled into an SD IRA?

Answer: IRAs, 401ks, Roth IRAs, SEP IRAs, 403bs, 457s, 401as, TSPs and profit-sharing plans like Keoghs—can be rolled over. The account can also be started with an initial contribution.

Roth and traditional funding in an IRA

Question: Can my IRA have both Roth and Traditional funds?

Answer: No. Roth and traditional money must be kept in separate IRAs. They are taxed (and therefore viewed) very differently by the IRS. Can both types be combined into one investment? Yes. (See chapter 12 on co-investing.)

Can one IRA LLC hold Roth and traditional?

Question: Can one IRA LLC hold both Roth and traditional money?

Answer: Yes, but it's not necessarily recommended. The reason is because whatever percentage you start the LLC with must remain for its lifetime, and if you want to make contributions or take distributions they must always follow that percentage. For example, you open the LLC rolling in $50k Roth and $50k Traditional, for $100k total. The next year you want to roll in an additional $25k from a Roth IRA. Well, you can't do that unless you have $25k in a Traditional IRA to put in.

Same thing with distributions. When you hit 70½ and, say, you must take $5k as a distribution. Well, you will have to take out $5k of your Roth IRA as well, even though otherwise you are not obligated to.

Therefore, although it can be done, it is not necessarily the best way to go. Even if you save some money in setup fees, you may find the limitations regarding contributions and distributions not worth the savings. We have found that the ideal scenario for this type of structure is when no additional funds are likely needed for the investment and the client will sell off the investment before ever needing to take a distribution.

Husband and wife, one IRA?

Question: Can husband and wife share one IRA?

Answer: No. The "I" in IRA stands for individual. She has hers, and he has his. Therefore, if a husband and wife want to roll over funds into an SD IRA they typically need two plans, one for each of them.

Credit cards allowed?

Question: Once my IRA LLC is set up, can I use a credit card to pay for expenses related to the real estate (or asset)?

Answer: No. A credit card is a type of personal guarantee, which is not allowed (see above, Chapter 11). Also, beware of credit card companies, which are always looking for new customers and often mail credit card applications to newly-formed businesses. If you receive a credit card application for the LLC, never fill it out or sign it because, by doing so, you will be issuing a personal guarantee on behalf of the LLC. Additionally, do not apply for overdraft protection or for a line of credit for your account, for the same reasoning.

On the other hand, you can use a debit card. Many clients, for instance, set up debit cards at the local Home Depot and charge all their purchases related to the IRA-asset on it.

Physical possession of precious metals?

Question: Can I take physical possession of precious metals (such as gold) with an SD IRA?

Answer: Precious metals are addressed in Section 408 of the US Tax Code. There you can find out exactly what kind of gold you may purchase for your Self-Directed IRA. From an IRS perspective, gold comes in two acceptable products: bullion bars and coins. Each of these possesses its own unique set of regulations.

Generally, bullion and many coins must be held by an approved depository through an IRA custodian, such as Brinks or the Delaware Depository. You can buy and sell it from there, but you can't take physical possession.

Whereas bullion bars and coins must generally be held by an approved custodian, gold/silver/platinum American Eagles may be held physically. A company offering an SD IRA (or Solo 401k) should be able to produce documentation pointing to the appropriate section in the IRS code. Ask them for it if you're skeptical.

*

Thanks for reading this book. Hopefully, you learned things you didn't know or at least now know what you don't know, and have an idea who to ask to get your questions answered. Feel free to post a review of it on Amazon.

For more information: www.broadfinancial.com

94078150R00040

Made in the USA
Middletown, DE
18 October 2018